A BOOK OF CHANGE

A BOOK OF CHANGE

Poems by FREDERICK MORGAN

WITH PAINTINGS BY HOZAN MATSUMOTO

New York / CHARLES SCRIBNER'S SONS

For Paula

The soul lives by that which it loves rather than in the body
which it animates. For it has not its life in the body,
but rather gives it to the body and lives in that which it loves.
                                        —ST. JOHN OF THE CROSS

The Valley Spirit never dies.
It is called the Mysterious Female,
and the doorway of the Mysterious Female
is the base from which Heaven and Earth spring.
It is there within us all the time.
Draw upon it as you will, it never runs dry.
                                        —LAO TZU

A BOOK OF CHANGE

ONE

A man must do his own believing, as he will have to do his own dying.

—LUTHER

I

Two birds are perched in the midnight tree.
One whistles, hops and preens
his golden plumage ceaselessly;
he can't think what he means.

The other—motionless, discreet—
watches with golden eyes
till their twin radiances meet
in the profound sunrise.

Dear son, your face came to me in a dream last night,
earnestly listening—or perhaps, about to put me a question—
pleasant and clear, bright-eyed in your intentness,
as so often I have seen you look in the old days.

And the pain stabbed me to the heart because even in the dream
I knew you were dead, and that I would never see you again,
never again have the joy of conversation with you,
my son whom I begot and always cherished.

This was the first time I could dream of you,
or perhaps, the first time I had the strength to remember,
and I thank God for it and for the pain and the tears—
May they open my heart to the depths of life and death.

III

Thinking of the past, and of crossroads
where a man meets, or does not meet, his time,
I wonder at my own old reckonings
and how a guidance came to stir in me—
grew like a plant nudging up green shoots
and thrusting nubby branchlets to the sun—
uncomfortable to the heart's strong customs
that moved the earlier life. On all roads now
the time draws near in the form of a man in green,
a man from the past whose body holds the future
in its live currents, being invisible
to those whose hearts have not suffered the growth—
but seen at last, a man to be embraced,
for he is you who read and I who write.

I V

Changeless themselves, the golden persons lurk
in the past, the fictive world, the fourth dimension,
not obviously there—but available
to the freshened heart that focuses its sight.
Each is a seed, a kernel of bright gold
that can be cracked and opened if you know how:
enormous dark within, and a thousand winds
raging to bring those blessings deeply feared
of choice and chance and joy and illumination.
Mark them, my soul—the general in his tent
ordering the line of battle for the morrow;
the lovers in the groves by Mytilene;
the prince who left his throne and searched for God:
not what they tell, but what is told in them.

V

I haste, dear Lord; I need not haste. Your arms,
sustaining each man's world of sense and mind,
hold us for ever: They the eternal hills
I sang of as a boy in the cold chapel
not knowing your most stern and tender love.
You hold my patient father, my first wife—
poor bitter child who never came to bloom—
and one of whom I still can scarcely speak:
my dear, dead, generous son. You hold us all—
the living too—and we, alive and dead,
make up one living mind, one suffering Self,
one being whom you love—perhaps a son—
in whom we move, as pain breaks into joy,
through obscure fates into your arms at last.

V I

How to tell you I love you?
Words wander off into silence,
unable to reach the full
victorious destination.

Words are travelers, busy
with problems of transportation,
often harassed and hurried.
There is peace, though, in the thought of arrival.

As on a spring day when the heart,
transfixed with the bliss of new life,
pauses—so pauses it now
as my words go groping for you.

VII

The splendid Person in the sun
who blessed my boyhood's intellect
when lying on the Greenwich lawn
I felt his presence clear-serene
beyond the countries of the clouds
tells me, dear Paula, you are my love—

The ancient Fisher in the moon
who pulls the tides past Singapore
and, friend of crabs, shows me in dreams
the crystal origins of words
and the glad life when man was young
tells me, sweet Paula, you are my love—

The Elephant who holds the world
and holds me, moving through deep sleep,
on his broad back and guards the lives
of all these beings moving on
cycle through cycle into bliss
tells me, good Paula, you are my love.

VIII

TO PAULA

My little one, my fair,
in you I've found my wealth:
in your deep eyes and hair
your richly blooming self.
Paula, I should despair
of knowing anywhere
but in your fragrant arms
the true pulse of my health—
My dearest one, my fair,
in you I've found myself.

22

GIFT OF A POEM

This child born of the small dark hours
is small herself and still unsure
of life, perhaps: not fully shaped.
Daylight will show us she is ours,

but who may know her finally
or tell whence comes her beating heart
or the charmed silence in her eyes?
Great Eros fathered her through me,

he who has given us our rich
and hidden life—whom we adore.
Take her, dear Paula, search her face,
find of his splendor one bright trace.

X

BARBERSHOP POEM

Slushed down Madison. The fog was lifting.
Barber quoted from Tom Paine
"These are the times that try men's souls."
(Governor's son picked up for pot.)
Bright bottles lined in a row before the mirror—
"What splendor! It all coheres."
Your life, my life, Tom Paine's life,
the sick, the sane, the unexplained life,
all lives emerge from the bright center
spoke after spoke on the golden wheel,
brothers and sisters on the wheel of becoming—

X I

Duck, riding the reservoir waves,
       ride the waves without fear.
The city is vast around you,
       the sky is clear.

The heart in its nest of feathers
       suffers mortality
locked by frail walls from the final
       chill of ecstasy.

Brokenly, at the luminous
       depths of my existence,
still I reckon the eternal
       waves' persistence—

Freshness of waters at the heart,
       though heart must fail and die,
unlocks the mind to plenitudes:
       city and vast sky.

XII

To live in the moment, each day as it comes,
requires a discipline and cleanliness:
it's not quite giving up hope, but hope becomes
an extension, merely, of the day's awareness,
not something set apart like a bank account
or accumulation of pledges falling due.
God speaks from the whirlwind: "Count on nothing at all
except that I will love and try you hard
and bring all things to an end, including you
as you have known yourself all these days past.
Your root is in me, child, and the root is here
always, and I am here at the golden heart
of each frail moment passing—always new.
It's death to cling to me, but life to find me."

XIII

THE PRISONER

It was in May, bright May,
in the long sweltering days
when lovers pay their court
to soft and willing maids:
alone and sad, I lay
locked fast in the deep keep
and never knew the nightfall
nor glad return of day
save for one little bird
who sang to me in the dawn.

A crossbowman came and shot her—
God strike him deaf and blind!

(From the Spanish, XVth Century, anonymous)

XIV

Lying naked on a granite shelf at the edge of Blue Hill Bay, the pitted surface harsh beneath my back, my face burned by the sun and cooled by the foam, I was visited by the threefold vision:

Of Man—like an incomprehensible insect—dismembering himself, encasing himself in fantasies of metal, scurrying, flying, burrowing, festering: swarming over the earth and beyond in continual mournful futile flight from himself and his place of rest—

Of the Girl of burning gold, fearful to touch, ecstasy beyond ecstasy to embrace: being fullness of earthlife, mind not mind, god-goddess, self and Other—

Of the vast responsive shores of death, where mute things speak, and the fulfilled souls assembled by Charon call and reply eternally in coiling numbers old as love's delight.

X V

In how many ways does God fulfill himself—
in the man who loves a woman and knows her flesh,
in the stricken man who suffers his grief alone,
in the man whose mind decides a difficult path
and him whose laughter carries past all thought.
Unequal fates are brought to one in God,
all will be shared—and alien fates as well:
the crystal's silent burning in the rock,
the twisted elm's patient, persistent growth,
the serpent's sleep, the frog's cool reverie,
elation of the sea-bird flying free
and the peace of cows and calves in evening fields.
Each fate lived out in sun or darkness yields,
beyond our peace and terror, the peace of God.

X V I

Birds
forming themselves
a beautiful line
it should be blue
or violet like those meadows
beyond Aldebaran where souls of birds
joyfully culminate forming themselves in beautiful lines
glistening sun colored glistening star colored
present birds are glorious too
simply living moving modestly
in gray Maine
skies bird
colored

XVII

White sky in the last light.
        Imminence of trees.
Pale birch-trunks among gray trunks of pine.

Black branchings on the white
        remoteness. Tracework.
Visible clusterings; division of leaves.

Backdrop of nothingness.
        Sharp-drawn before it,
these bold complexities of present growth:

Time's strange distraction
        black as ink on paper
against the blankness of the unconditioned.

XVIII

Very high
against a primal blue shimmer of nothing
quiescent

as at the tip of a long blue branch of thought
from which depend blue shoots and scrolls of leafage—

cunning, too,
to the core of his head which blue may never
penetrate—

perches my tanager, of ultimate Red.

XIX

Somewhere there is a heaven that resembles
my idea of Cambridge sixty years ago:
long days of spring, tall elms, unhurried youths,
huge halls of soft stone aging in the sun.
Or not a heaven, but a resting place,
along a farther road some of us follow,
meant for instruction, where the quiet soul
learns for a time the wisdom of not doing.
In a great mess-hall underneath dim flags
I sat at table between you, my good friends—
you, priestly at the head, eating and smiling,
you at my right, extending gentle hands—
in dream. Yes, but it was our three real selves
at a meeting-place where they may always meet.

X X

When a loved person dies, and we see the courage,
patience, humor, warmth all gone for good
along with the little ways we knew and loved,
how can we bear the terror and the pain?
We know the world's at fault, and so is God—
if he made the world—for nothing that's so fine
should be made to suffer miseries and die.
And yet that fineness became all the finer
throughout the suffering, in us and him,
and the love stronger, for there is a link.
Dear brothers, sisters, knowing ourselves mortal,
let us cherish each other always, joining
living and dead in the golden chain of love.
Then God may say: "This, you and I have made."

XXI

Child, you will die; but between that breath and this—
now at this moment, unless you put her off—
eternity outspreads her glittering fields
where animals play and rivers dance in the sun:
mostly invisible to the time-bent mind,
accessible not through time but through the tasting
of golden fruit that ripens soon or late
or maybe never, in a given life.
We all stand equidistant from the center—
the glowing, sacred center—and all are saved
(if we but knew it) and all must suffer pain
and die the real death and lose our selves
late or soon, in terror, to find our Selves
that walk those quiet meadows even now.

I saw my darling on the street
walking home with clothes in her arms—
clothes from the cleaners—she walked along
past where the school was being built

on the next block. I called to her—
shouting "Paula!" out my window.
Shouted twice, three times. A black
construction worker grinned at me

from the unfinished roof. My dear one
turned, looked back the way she'd passed,
then—as I called again—looked up,
saw me, and smiled, and called: "I'm coming!"

Earlier on the telephone
we had spoken to a dying friend
in a suburban hospital.
A loving voice, but very faint.

God takes our friends in death. He gives
us pains to match (at least) our joys.
But gives, too, moments in each day
in which the heart may find itself

and learn its freedom in the vaster
gift of love in which it breathes.
Just as my heart is learning now—
my heart in which her smile still blooms.

XXIII

Dear Agnes, you were dying and you knew it.
We stood there. One at each side of the bed
looked down at you who smiled still through your pain.
You held each with a hand, and said: "You two
are surely happy, you're looking so damn well,"
and gave the hands a squeeze. Well, we smiled back,
holding our tears, and told you that we were
happy indeed, and tried to share it with you.
Perhaps we did, because later on you said,
"If we just keep on loving, we'll come out right."
That is a message I've thought of often since,
for when we left you (the last time, and we knew it)
we brought with us the blessing of your words
and your last look that will not be forgotten.

XXIV

Oh Lord, one knows no longer how to name you,
but you are still my God, the master of all life,
whom after years of search I have begun to find;
who has found me, rather; or rather, never lost me.

(For you are more than can be found. As Lao Tzu said,
the farther one travels, the less one ends up knowing;
by keeping still and letting the great winds blow
one may prepare oneself to hear your voice.)

At this fresh dawn in the middle of my life—
youth recaptured with its joys and sparkling plumage,
the ten thousand gleamings seen with steadier eyes,
the fragrance tasted more fully in evanescence—

steady my steps along the road,
help me abate my rage and fretfulness,
this energy of yours, help me control it!
Strong and in order let the good words sound.

Let thoughts be of earth, of love and of dear friends,
and of her in whom I hold my joy and youth—
each day praising you that you brought her to me—
let thoughts be of earth, our mother whom we must cherish.

One need not speak of you each day, each hour,
but let each day, each hour be a prayer to you,
each sacred instant—oh, creator destroyer
preserver of all that is loved: master and friend.

XXV

Why father children? Once upon a time
a son or daughter was a part of the self
extended into the future, that slowly grew
and shaped itself and coalesced, becoming
one and separate as it reached full growth—
a different self at last. And this was painful,
but with a gradual, familiar pain
that one could accept as natural, and bear.
But now, the break is total and abrupt
and each one grows (or not) in his own place;
indeed, we have no future in our children
nor do we count in theirs (if they conceive one).
All—naked—wait the future of the world.
It's father to none, then—or else, father to all.

XXVI

Across far lands and oceans where you've passed,
    Veronica Morgan,
through days and nights in changeless alternation,
behind whatever walls you wake and sleep,
I think of you as of a life that's mine
    and yet not mine, dear daughter.

Children seem frail and tender, and are so,
    Veronica Morgan,
in those first years. A father suffers, cares,
decides, and takes a life into his hands
and from that weakness builds himself a self
    that may not be his true one.

Yes, fathers must learn to release their children,
    Veronica Morgan,
to life, to death, to whatever destiny
is theirs alone by right of lot and choice.
Hard, to give up protecting; but protecting
    is not the same as loving.

My destiny is mine, yours is your own,
    Veronica Morgan,
and each, as he will have to live his dying,
must live his living too. And thence comes freedom,
the breathing-in of the full strength of life
    though in the end it kill us.

I tell you now your life is yours entirely,
    Veronica Morgan,
your joy, your chance. Remember me as father
only as father changes shape to friend:
friend at the root, and in life's mystery
    perhaps to be found again.

XXVII

MEMORIES OF CAMP HOOD

1

North Camp Hood in 1943.
A grid of rectangles clamped down on mud.
Barracks, mess halls, motor-parks, latrines
rigid and raw in the bland Texas light.

Something was wrong with the people who could make
that. Something still is. . . . An obsessed haste
to "do what has to be done" (always an illusion)
is used to justify the squalid waste.

Wars were said to justify all things;
it's clearer now there's nothing justifies
ugliness, cruelty. . . . Money was made, of course,
and green things beaten flat into the ground.

—Those months in headquarters, we lived off post,
rose up from warmish beds and smell of wives
into chill morning air at 5:00 A.M.
and drove our car-pool, each his day in turn—

Ross, Ogden, Schaeffer, Carmody and I—
back to dull hell through the soft freshening dawn.
It was a fate we wouldn't recognize
and we told jokes on the way as the sun came up.

There was a glint in the air, a desert smell,
a quickening sense almost like alcohol
over the stark land. I felt the future in it
and gave myself to the oncoming day.

—It seems it's of himself that man builds hell
from which he keeps on trying to escape:
of the self he's not—fearing the self he is.
Sometimes it's good to know there will be an end!

But always the desert remains, and the desert light,
and this *I am* that holds those days in its heart,
reflections of hell and something more enduring. . . .
The scent of sage-brush rises still to my nostrils.

   2

Reinhart, I've thought of you from time to time
for almost thirty years now, how to that
parched ugly man-made geometric waste
where we poor damned slaved and endured our days
you brought your touch of decency and reason.
You didn't fear your strength, but used it well:
ready to hear each man to the end, you held
compassion and authority in balance.
Yes, Sergeant Reinhart, justice lived in you.

And you next, Sergeant Weaver, come to mind,
a woman in the army! slim and blonde
and bitter-hard. We worked together six months
stand-offishly with mutual respect.
One didn't try to come too close to you—
still, once or twice, the woman warmly showed.
You wrote me a letter, after you shipped out,
extending friendship at last, with news and jokes.
I never answered it: forgive me that.

Sergeant Granowski, now a word for you,
who worked with me for the post psychiatrist,
the biggest fool that you or I had met.

You typed his cases, listened to his rant,
and—with your worried, somewhat doglike look—
tried, when you had the chance, to help sick men.
You had a false tooth that screwed in and out,
and when we ate together in the mess hall,
removing it, you would apologize.

Then, Sergeant Reid, you: elegant, refined,
your uniform creased always to knife-edge,
your manner smiling, friendly and composed.
I see you now—coming to call on me!—
crossing the dismal lot outside my "office"
bland and serene as though you were home in Boston
on a Sunday afternoon. What poise you had!
We'd sit and talk a while of Henry James,
or Milton, whom we both read in those days.

And you last, Sergeant Freeman, first name "Armo,"
friend, bunk-mate, farm boy from Louisiana,
we had nothing at all in common but
one big thing: a deep liking, man for man,
and understanding gained without much talk.
When orders came one day that made me sergeant,
you wrote at the top, "You is a good man, Morgan!"
—Where are you, Freeman? Did you go back home?
What was your destiny in life, or death?

3

Miss Corporal Mazzard—
so pretty, no wizard
could spell all your charms
from his *A* to his izzard—

you had a wide grin and
two little plump titties
that you kept neatly covered
(the more was the pity):

I tried to seduce you
but it was unavailing,
you scurried clean off
with a shrieking and wailing . . .

—For your pretty soul, Mazzard,
I've kept on a-praying:
on the hazardous desert
may you never go straying

and wander off lost
and fall limp as a lizard
and feel the slow buzzard
come nibble your gizzard.

4   (Driving through Venus, Texas)

Yes, spirit of this place; but not in your Cyprian guise
as when you rose from the white foam chaste as shell
with glistening shoulders, slick abdomen, droplets in
   your hair
and the sea's serenity on your new-shaped face.

Open-mouthed, you stare across gray, scrubby plains,
a broken shack behind you, a slum of wash on the line
and all is dust, grit, loneliness. . . . Quiet, though,
   beneath cheap cloth
huge girlish bubbies tell me who is here.

5

Anne, since I wrote that poem for your birthday
more years have turned than you or I had lived,
and I have lost you utterly, and care
no more for you than for a thousand others
remembered now with vague benevolence,
shapes in my life; indeed, you're more remote,
perhaps because I never saw you squarely
but always through a haze of sick desire.
In that old war, for a few weeks, I loved you,
yearned to touch you, kiss you, hold you naked,
and now—I scarcely can recall your face.
I found that poem tonight, weak and pretentious,
scrawled on a scrap of thirty-year-old paper,
and burned it; and wrote this one in its place.

6   (New Year's Day, 1945)

Sudden descent from sulky Texas skies—
a cardinal appeared in our back yard
that morning. We felt certain of our luck.
He hopped through our dead garden and went away.

At noon it cleared. We visited some friends
who had an ugly, screaming, new-born child.
They were the boring kind: I've lost their names.
Of course, we too had something in the pot.

Driving through the slow light of afternoon
we saw an empty schoolhouse in the fields;
climbed out, walked over, peered into the windows,
saw the rich glow of sun on varnished chairs.

There was stillness, there was the sacred quiet
where man and woman might know present life.
Swallows were darting over the late fields
but we took thought of night and going home.

The emptiness, the beauty, were all there,
but we were not yet ready, were we, dear?
Nor were you ever ready, poor dead wife:
you had six children, never your own life.

Your body, which my body knew, is gone.
My body, which still holds those days within,
moved to other women, other lives,
and for a little longer yet, goes on.

—A month passed, then in distant, dim New York
she died who was the fortress of my youth,
an old, proud woman.—Then came pain and fear,
change after change releasing me to now.

XXVIII

The serpent of the shadows crept
into my thoughts in '27.
The butler from the house next door
showed me his penis, long and red.

I read of whales and dinosaurs
in the *Book of Knowledge,* rainy days,
and woke up screaming one hot night
fearing hell and my evil nurse.

Dad commuted from New York,
played golf, kept up with the Stock Exchange.
Mother waited on the grandparents.
The boy was left pretty much alone

and the nation drove to a kind of end.
Everywhere, though, new seeds are sown:
strange, this link of the what-I-was
to mortal breaths I'm breathing now!

God slays himself with each new year
but the purusha dwells unseasoned.
Friends, your every heaven and hell
are threaded with autumnal rains.

—We killed the snake with a garden shovel,
innocent beast of darting tongue.
The days moved on. We moved with them.
I stand here now and write this poem.

Scotch Mary lived in the kitchen with the *News*.
I was afraid of her. She wore old, broken shoes,
was huge and shapeless, her hair in a frowsy bun.
Often she chased me out of the kitchen fast
but sometimes let me sit at the zinc-topped table
where she drank her coffee with the papers outspread
and read about rich people and the bad things they did.

One summer afternoon the ceiling fell
somewhere in the back. A great crash. I cried out,
not thinking, "Mary! Where's Mary?" No one was hurt.
But she came from her little room and held me tight
against her until I gasped. "God bless the child!
He thought of old Mary, he thought of old Mary," she said.

X X X

Boy and spirit traveled in a clock
over the frosted town on Christmas Eve:
the speaking animals were bundled warm
in earthy burrows under drifted snow.

His house left far behind, the objects in it
took on, in distance, strange lives of their own
not threatening, but firm: they were his equal.
He felt more kin to the rabbit and the deer.

The spirit laughed and beckoned to the future:
bright colors, sugared scents, tastes in profusion
suddenly spread out a patchwork landscape.
Everywhere, though, a tiny malice lurked

as if to warn him only (not defeat him);
it's not so hard to tell the good from the bad—
but to tell good from good, now that's the trick!
When he returned—in safety?—it was Christmas.

XXXI

FOR PAULA   (December 22, 1970)

First day of snow.
                    A celebration!
to walk in the briefly beautiful streets.
This morning we are separated, only for a time;
you follow one path, I another
                    through the white city.
Down beneath, at the roots of things, we are together.
I think of you, of your smile, your direct joy in life,
your goodness that makes life radiant all about you.
Soon I shall see you, soon our paths converge:
the one life pursuing its destined and sacred way.

XXXII

THE SMILE

(TO PAULA)

"She walks in beauty," Byron wrote:
a beauty, though, somewhat unreal—
it's what he thought he should have felt,
perhaps, and not what he did feel.

Doubtless, he loved. And doubtless, too,
a poem may exaggerate;
but this small one I'm writing you,
Paula my love, will tell it straight.

I sat here in my chair, eyes closed,
waiting for a poem to come;
half-sleeping, from my depths I heard
your movements in the other room.

Opened my eyes a crack, and saw
you fixing flowers in our green vase:
African daisies fresh from Holland,
purple and red anemones.

Your hands were deft. Your face, intent
above that work you do so well,
took on a gentle, abstract smile.
That smile is more than poems can tell,

is the true beauty, grace of one
at home with her desires and powers.
I treasure it, and always shall,
that smile of yours above the flowers.

XXXIII

Dear Wanderer, on your unimagined journey
I see you pause one night at a scene like this—
a tiny town, four or five houses only
clustered along the shore of a frozen lake
looked over by the white church from its hill.
It's old New England, it may be Christmas Eve,
the ground is covered white and deep with snow;
outside the Inn three carolers are singing,
all bundled warm against the frosty night,
but folks are mostly home eating their suppers,
while the horses snort and steam in the warm barns.

I see you in white cloak and hood, apart,
standing in snow where you have left no track.
The stars are out, the air is bitter cold.
With a faint smile, you recognize the scene,
rejoicing (you rejoice in all things now),
but have no need to hold it or possess it.
Detached and loving, ready now to leave,
you linger long enough to smile once more
at two plump children tumbling on the ice.

XXXIV

Cold night in Princeton, 1942.
Dark sky with cloud-shapes, here and there a star,
the air freezing. I wore no overcoat
and whistling to myself "Blues in the Night"
passed through the dark quadrangles edged with snow.

My mind surged forward through the cloudy years—
what would they bring me? First of all, a war,
obscurity of shifting hopes and fears.
But looked beyond, and saw some kind of end
where things would be once more what I had known.

Never to be. The past remains the past,
retains the magic of what's left behind
and makes illusion of its afterglow;
the present moves into the unforeseen,
creates its living magic as it goes.

A war, a wife and children, then a life—
a sense, not false, of doing what I ought
and what I wanted: it was quite sincere
but just a bit rebellious, as though forced—
life sprang its trap, I wasn't where I thought.

A quarter of a century to learn
through pain, and loss, and gain, to find myself
in joy that links me to the one I was.
Sharer of my joy, we heard that tune last night:
here, where I am, I offer you this poem.

X X X V

In the frozen winter
far from Bethlehem
ice cracks on the sordid ponds
of this my land that once was fair.

Cold winds move the poisons
through the sullen sky
over cities where men clot
in shifting millions in the streets.

Christmas is approaching.
We seek homes in time:
somewhere warmth of a loved face
or the dear body whom we've held.

Goodness is of persons:
two, or three, or four,
loving, sharing, bearing with;
evil's abroad, outside the door,

covering each corner
of despairing earth—
field and forest, mountain, sea—
with stinking discharge of man's pride.

Goodness is corrupted
(mystery profound):
evil is of persons too,
else would our garden not be fouled.

Jesus, naked baby
tossed up on the straw,
have we followed you so far,
to this last abomination?

With your sword of doctrine
have you severed us,
good within from good without,
given us power in place of love?

Jesus, in your image
of a naked babe,
tender from your mother's womb,
clasped to her breast as she smiles down,

I see still the emblem
of the wished-for world:
where man is nature's lover,
where beasts and angels are at home.

XXXVI

FOR PAULA

Gentle Paula,
      little dove,
dearer than dear and closer than close,
how may I praise our love in words?
What words are there so deep?

I'll hold you then,
      dawn and dusk,
body to body closer than close,
until the Word from our world within
utters our depths of love.

*

The clouds scud through the sky tonight
riding a wind from the sea,
the world is vast and fresh outside—
while inside, we

sit in the warm room we love
where Love has made us one,
readying our quiet souls
for him to come.

*

*Your body in my arms is
your breast beneath my hand is
my body in your body is*

*Love is the bed that bears us
Love is the room that holds us
Love is the life that forms us*

*

A dawn breeze stirs
the window-shades,
light pales
on the vast city.

We wake. We touch.
We clasp each other:
your body soft
and fair in my arms.

Another day:
sacred, not
for what it means
but for what it is.

XXXVII

Sometimes I hear my father's voice, sometimes my son's, in mine:
the modulations of two who have died—
passing beyond these tides of being. Gone,

but still their forms appear as though in sudden shafts of sun:
Dad in the corner chair at "39"
smoking his pipe; John standing at my desk

smiling, talking to me of school, or work, or politics.
Both of them are real to me today,
more real than half the people whom I meet,

as if their being, somehow, is in very loss confirmed.
Reality may be a being in mind
and who knows at what point the mind has end?

The world that is not here may be a world of sun and trees,
a world of man's potentialities:
our absences may there be presences.

Perhaps, in the long run, all mind, all memory is shared
just as the body's basic stuff is shared
that crumbles and renews, as time moves on

(illusive time—whose motion may be but a long day's dream!)
in other bodies, other being. Yes,
likely we are one substance, of which mind,

matter, are forms. Voices of past and future speak in ours
and somewhere, all is known—as I know now
father's and son's reality in me.

XXXVIII

The ten thousand things are getting out of hand,
may be headed for the ultimate smashup?

Let them go, let them be,
seeming is not the same as being.

There is a responsibility to the contingent.
Accept it, but remain true to the center,

for the central point is greater than any sphere,
and the Way is there, as it has always been.

Do these two things: you are a sage.
Only begin to do them: you are freed from hysteria,

from the diseased commotion of the age—
free to act cleanly, without regret or apprehension.

Above all, do not use man to help out heaven
or your mind, to help out what you cannot know.

Be yourself, as an old misshapen tree
is itself whether living or dead or beyond life and death.

Then you may move among the myriads
invulnerable, and play your part as well.

XXXIX

In the fair Bermudas
they live in fearlessness,
naked and strong-legged
in many-colored headdresses.

While pears drop from the trees
and crabs climb the still beach,
they plunge through beating surf
to spear fat fish that flounder in.

They move in calm arenas
of pleasure, pain, and rest,
take each as it arrives,
meeting it with the full person—

not shifting miserably
in search of distant goals.
Thus when death comes in turn
they find that he, too, is the best.

X L

Whatever I may be, or think, or do,
I offer all of it, great God, to you,
not to relieve myself of the hard choice
of answering each call in my own voice,
nor to evade responsibility
of tasting the day's joy or misery
wholeheartedly, in all my depths of self—
but, God, because I feel you are my Self,
all that I have been, all that I will be,
the secret strength, the hidden potency
and far, far more—for you are all else, too,
and the great wind of freedom blowing through.
You're other, I can't know you; but your voice
sings to my living depths, and I rejoice.

XLI

One life: its extremes and every point between—
one weave, one fabric, one consistency,
whether I sorrow or whether I rejoice.
Waking beside Paula, holding her close;
kneeling on the floor to say my morning prayers;
hoisting the blinds, looking outside at the day;
eating my breakfast; shaving and taking a crap;
reading the papers; walking downtown with my stick . . .
One life: remembering my children when they were small
and I read or told them stories after supper;
one life: weeping inside for my son who's dead;
one life: thanking God for his force within
that drove me to find my love, my destiny,
my future opening now ahead: one life.

TWO

*Dark and hidden, the Way seems not to exist and yet it is there;
lush and unbounded, it possesses no form but only spirit. . . .*

—CHUANG TZU

I

IMAGINARY EPITAPHS

1

What was unimportant
he held at arm's length,
incurred a hatred
proportioned to his strength

Knew never the taste
of joy at its root,
knew the hard comfort
of the word's pursuit

Lived in his hope
and *acted* to the end,
died on a cold night
leaving one or two friends.

2

He lies between the airport and
                 the machine-tool factory,
where a dim crowd of slabs is hemmed
                 among the hindered trees.

His emptied heart—by day by night—
                 hums to the whining cars
while a blank angel strews his dirt
                 with nonexistent tears.

3

Here where he lies, the grasses
reach to the gray sky with a wry determination:

coarse, harsh, spiky,
in the acrid redolence of integrity.

He has made the ground his own—
and heaven may yearn, but not exceed this justice.

I I

There are no peacocks in my house,
the peacocks stride on the lawns;
there are no swans in my strong house,
the lake is clouded with swans.

But dreams of peacocks and of swans
ascend, descend the marble stairs
and moonlight on the terraces
portends blonde girls in whirling gowns.

A dream of dancers in the snow
(the swans are frozen on the lake)
whirls through the house at 10:00 P.M.,
but the clear windows may not break

to fling the dancers out-of-doors
or let the cocks come striding in:
proud cocks would faze the gossamer girls,
their colors rasp my pearly floors.

The swan-necks peck at the slick quick legs
of white girls whisking through the snows—
the strong house glints in the long moonlight
and wakes at dawn to the scrawls of crows.

III

In stillest air above the tableland
beats the transparent heart that prophesies
emblems of pure song prouder than all sound.

. . . In flux and reflux of systaltic tides
the dawn-wind sweeps the thistled fields and drives
my gray blood pulsing through the speechless skies
towards the city of the cold.

I V

In the world of purple light
the people are all plumed in white:
they float and flutter, dart and play,
and plunge into the sapphire spray
of their secret, inland seas.

One winter night in '35
I found my way there still alive.
Beloved New York was filled with mist,
her rainy pavements gleaming moist
beneath the street-lamps' yellowing—

At the dark edge of Washington Square
I found the path that leads elsewhere
and followed where it disappears.
Through every change of changing years
beneath the stones that path remains.

An earth turned strange; a sun subdued,
sifting through mists its colored moods
upon still forests and heavy grass
where the white beings turn and pass
in their unhindered solitudes—

They're blissful, but they're self-contained
from never having known our pain,
nor can we guess how they may love.
Like glad somnambulists they move
as though their stupor were from God.

I looked for a human-seeming face
or one that held at least some trace
of suffering— but there was none
in all that vast communion.
So I returned to my own place.

V

With unimpeded motion the swan glides forward into the polar dawn. His memories are washed clean of vehemence. His mind, bearing of his past only the pure outline, is white as his present plumage—through which an arctic wind sifts and filters. On all sides vast perspectives of ice begin to sparkle with the first premonitions of day. August is forgotten: Leda and her coral flesh, the richness of summer greens. A great cold breath invades and exhilarates his heart.

V I

The love of the jaybird for the rose
is a fearsome thing, in chilly spring,
the love of the jaybird for the rose
aggrieves my heart—and I walk apart
and the light wind lifting slim treetops
perturbs my heart, and I walk apart
dreaming of filth by the harborside
in smoky ports, and of boats that toss
amid the filth of the harborside
when the dark descends and day's work ends
in a draggle of cripples and muddy brats
when the dark descends and talking ends
and along the inland avenues
lamps are aglow in the calm windows
of mansions on broad avenues
where women with nipples sharp as spears
dance on the creamed and frozen floors—
the women with nipples sharp as spears
dance beneath glinting chandeliers
while their blank and bowing cavaliers
babble beneath the chandeliers. . . .

Christ! but the heart is a living thing
in despite of beauty and fine sayings
Christ! but the heart is a living thing.
Gargantua hoists his cock-and-balls
to the airs of spring, to the airs of spring,
Gargantua hoists his cock-and-balls,
takes on all comers, snorting fire,
the Phoenix rises from his pyre,
scorching the zenith with his fire,
and hurtles across Arabian space,
a meteor rises in the west,
hurtles across Arabian space

and lo! the Man is born again,
the tameless, blameless, featherless one,
Gargantua is born again
in a world of convicts and croaking crows,
drinks from his mother and blows his nose
in the world of convicts and croaking crows
and where he comes from nobody knows,
he loves the bluejay, he loves the rose,
but where he comes from, nobody knows. . . .

I bow to you, amazing Spring,
sweet rutting bitch of life and change,
I bow to you, amusing Spring,
and walk in quiet through your groves
holding my deep self in my heart
secretive as your shaded groves,
to an archaic waterfall
whose glittery chill awakes my sight.
There by the fabled waterfall
while a bird sends forth his clearest note
from treetops of returning green,
while a bird sounds forth his clearest note
I learn that Winter never dies—
timeless behind the moment's gleam—
I see that Winter never dies:
the frozen Star burns without sound
but light and heat must have an end,
the frozen Star burns without sound
and moveless, wordless night descends
when mind retreats beneath the ground
and at the last a night descends.

. . . Inspired one, I see your Eye
that watches from the generous sky,
inspired One, I see your "I"—
master of sunlight and of shit
at home in death and bones and grit,

master of sunlight and of shit
year-long I praise your cosmic verve,
gabbling away my muddy psalms,
year-long I praise your comic verve!
Then, great one, speak to me of life
in blaze of sun, in blast of storm,
tell me, my great one, of your life,
belch up your fogs, piss down your rains,
fart out your thunderous refrains,
belch up your fogs, piss down your rains,
and all your legends I shall sing
to these most frivolous airs of spring
your grandest stories I shall sing
to the fresh day awakening,
of your high glories I shall sing
and of my glad awakening.

VII

A touch of thyme is poignant on the air
and the taste of time is pungent to my sense
in this sea-garden where the rooks at evening
lavish their majesty of darkened knowledge.
While a salt breath implicit in the foliage
resumes the fervor of an old bereavement,
my heart at its clear center still retains
the scent of the verbena, sharp and rare.

For in the backwards garden of first morning
I knew a living dawn on bulb and blade
where dragonflies swerved vibrant in the gleam.
Time walked beside me, demi-god in green—
the sun reserved his ironies of shade—
the wind breathed tentatives that shaped no warning.

VIII

Coolness, and the heads of palms dipping in the sun-bright wind;
white walls, and empty shores, and an ocean sighing round—
the men and women moved with equanimity
but strange constellations blazed at night presumptuously.

Mornings I roamed the interior, uplands of bone and chalk;
watched the smooth topaz insects clenched to the dry salt stalks;
always a giant shadow followed, sycophant Beast—
tamed ageless dragon of death gulled of his vacuous feast.

But a young Dryad it was, slender in her first bloom,
whose limpid heart outspelled the wisdom of warm afternoons:
with green books in our hands— enigmas, bestiaries—
we sat at the sea's edge, our bare feet licked by the sea.

Then at dim of day I climbed the seven and seventy steps
to the Wizard's tower of stone, where he unchained his maps,
plotting remote disasters in the abstracted sky
while the mute starshine brimmed his undeclining eye.

Later I took dark rest upon my scaffold bed,
the night sky— purest creature— unscrolled above my head,
while at my feet the cunning Emblem of desire
crouched, she-shadow of voracious fur and fire.

But a sun dawned at last that bespoke me castaway:
sparless I floated on the swallowing wave, in chilly spray.
What landfall could remain, what rock face fronting the sea?
. . . Paradise and its phantoms fade in the day of destiny.

I X

Before the attempts of dawn, the horns made echo along
        the savage barbed ravines to the east of the city,
which uprose in the mid-distance classic but depleted, pallid in
        a fine-spun mist. And the birds,
the lithe birds whistled abruptly out of thickets (flowering now
        with small waxy stars of red and yellow)
where hatefully, nocturnal lovers had crouched, fulfilling their
        rituals and abominations.

The air was tensed in fineness, to the bristly scent of wood-herbs
        and rank sedge, when innocently the damp dawn breeze
brought near that gold nostalgia of horns and the hounds' black
        muttering; then knowledge filled me— standing
silent beneath the dwarf hemlock in a dawning lucidity of
        impulses and possibilities—
of the murderous and exalted night through which a man (or the
        pure ghost of a man) was hunted.

For I saw that formed fatality ascending— speechless, glanceless—
        the slopes of these forbidden gulches; falling,
rising again elegantly detached from stone and bramble, elect,
        unyielding and unbleeding:
I loved and pitied him; until— in the yellow light's more full
        assertion— he vanished, and the horns of chase
withdrew, and still I stood— unchanging and confirmed—
        alone in an evil land but free for ever.

X

Before the dawn men dream of shapes of ships.
The women beside them softly part their lips;
the children sleep—their sleep spreads deep beneath
cradle and house, where the sea-bottom heaves.
The houses crouch like cats in the dawn mist,
the cats roam, big as houses, on the hills
and in back yards ashcans by twos and threes
raise a loveless lament in the darkling breeze.

Brisk on the bay, the waves roll in bright-capped
to the brackish beach where kelp and shells are heaped.
The men with pails stroll downhill to the docks
in the brilliant air—their wives watch their slow backs—
and soon sharp echoes rise, quick-multiplied,
of mallets rapping from the harborside
while the soft mist lifts slowly in the heat
from chalky hills bestrewn with frowsy sheep.

High noon: the Sun is bellowing like a bull.
He fills the womb with gold, with honey the skull,
and smells of greenness rise from the fresh ground
where worms delve damply in their solemn rounds.
By white-fenced yards the warm bees dart and drone:
they skim the face of the boy who naps alone
while the sun-drenched Rose luxuriously distends
her fragrant cup to the wind's light finger-ends.

The supplest lovers couple after supper,
they grapple, happily, behind the chapel;
others, less purposefully nerved by lust,
chat on their porches in the purple dusk.
The baby sleeps alone: his mind gropes deep
along the ocean floor where great crabs creep,
and men with women twined lie on their beds.
Dreams of the wide sea move in their still heads.

XI

TRIOLETS

1

I slept with Ethelberta
one night in January.
It did not disconcert her
that I slept with Ethelberta . . .
Wishing —oh, not to hurt her!
but only to be merry—
I slept with Ethelberta
one night in January.

2

Astride the narrow ditch
Ruth raised her skirt to piss.
She felt a pleasing itch
astride the narrow ditch
and while birds at high pitch
whistled in their bliss,
astride the narrow ditch
Ruth raised her skirt to piss.

3

The bears at the South Pole
are paler than the moon.
They move without a goal,
those bears at the South Pole,
each sends his misty soul
before him through the gloom.
The bears at the South Pole
are paler than the moon.

4

I kissed the tangled hair—
I licked the salty skin
of shoulders sleek and bare,
I kissed her tangled hair
and told her she was fair,
Mathilde, as I thrust in.
I kissed the tangled hair
and licked the tender skin.

XII

ILLUMINATIONS

1

The princess from her couch at dawn
     sings to the sun
that he may fill her with his joy
     of battles won,

of a perfection that foretells
     the pyramids
and wisdom that may bid the Sphinx
     close his worn lids,

for there is nothing that she knows
     or may not know
but the *within* which from the god's
     darkness must grow

as she moves on in quietude
     down branching days,
his gold still coursing through her blood's
     unspoken ways,

until in the deep stone at last
     her visions cease
to be but hers—and make return
     to their first peace.

2

At noon, the furry girls stretch out and talk about fucking
and pat themselves and laugh and touch their fuzzy places.
A wind from the Aegean brings brine against the olives.
Somewhere is an eye: in the thyme, maybe, or jasmine.

From the leaves a memory glints: of keen Odysseus,
the wanderer who is to come in crafty rectitude—
full of thought, enduring—one who knows his destiny
and in despite of gods makes it his destination.

Can the beast-girls recall the weathered skin of the hero,
or is it some vague foretaste that distends their furry lips,
or yet—in the pure caldron—do they see time's ways all one:
outer and inner being of the great god-and-goddess?

For what are rest and action? Gods in the leaf and blossom,
gods in the sea-spray and storm, oppose us and uphold us,
and all of us weave the web: the spider bids us remember
ever the wanderer has the gray-eyed one at his side.

Does it come to the same thing, then—all that strong journeying,
and lassitude of passive bodies in the hot noon sun?
If Odysseus remains, the god is in the fucking;
if he leaves, it is the god within who moves him on.

3

The Arabian came to me "gowned in white."
Outside the city walls we lay all night.
Dry season—and mid-Asiatic hush:
my pearls glowed damply in the blackish bush

and melons hung full to my tasting lips.
I tasted them, and took long gentle sips
of tarter berries lurking soft below—
then learned how deeply my own roots could grow.

The moon above us was a coin of gold.
The treetops moved to a design foretold
by old geometers of Babylon
who knew which edge of being they were on.

Here—inner, outer, male and female merge—
and day and night—in the blind stunning urge
that brings new wisdom at its desperate term.
I lay back on the earth weak as a worm,

stricken with the dark gift of deeper being,
then—looking up—with that dark double seeing
beheld the huge clouds coursing through the sky:
gods, goddesses; bearers of destiny.

XIII

PAGES FROM A FORGOTTEN BOOK

1

After passing through deserts where thousands had left their bones, I came at last to the untouched lake on which the swan with diamond eyes floated unconcerned. One glance of challenge: I lowered my head peaceably. Then followed her through margin reeds as she led me into the forest, where a small house awaited me in the enduring green.

2

Naked, with full udders swinging, the savage woman crawled through the earthy underbrush. The forest was damp after rain, wet leaves adhering to the dark soil. I caught her and mounted her; after the spasm I saw, looking into her eyes, that I had known her centuries before: in another life, as another woman.

3

Beyond mountains, beyond cities, in a land uninhabited by men (who lose their way in search of it) there lies a quiet inland sea. An orchard stretches along its shores: mile after mile of rustling fragrance, where birds and animals live hiddenly. All kinds of trees grow here, but only a single peach, from which hangs a single fruit. He who eats the peach and cracks the pit between his jaws will pass from himself through himself, through the last blackness into knowledge.

4

In the forgotten castle's ruined court
we stand, a knot of travelers out of time
awaiting the fulfillment of the word
spoken in time's dawn, when all things breathed.

Now, the lizard scuttles on broken flags
and dark reversion stills the forest air
until the evening hints a sudden gleam:
a glint of gold that hovers faintly down.

Bright breast-plume of a kestrel or a hawk,
catching the sun's last light, it floats, it falls,
and writes a message in the ancient dust:
The life to come is but your breathing now.

5

Come out! Come out! little girl, said the button-man. I have sewn buttons all over my clothes—blue ones, yellow ones, red ones, green ones. They are useless, and so I have no cares, and am happy. Come live with me, walk with me through the world, and I shall sew buttons all over your frocks, and we shall be happy together for ever.

In the forest of civilized beasts, only the people were wild.
The animals governed them, with wisdom and forbearance. One
day a man, who had been running through the woods hitting and
hurting every living being in his path, was brought before his
judge, an elephant. "Why don't you kill me?" he challenged. "For
I would kill all of you animals gladly in order to obtain what is
more precious to me than life itself, my freedom!" "No," replied
the judge, "we animals refuse to adopt your human values in these
matters, and consider that your penchant for reducing life and
death to *extremes* proves you to be a deformation of nature." And
he sentenced him to six months' silence and meditation, in the
custody of the grizzly bear.

In his tree-house, high above the fields and forests of his
father's little kingdom, the young prince felt far removed from the
concerns of court and from the necessity of pleasing his parents.
Here he could read all day, dream, let his mind wander; he enjoyed
a nearly perfect freedom. But one evening, when he descended, he
found his parents murdered, his palace in ruins, his country
burned and pillaged by barbarian invaders. He was alone with the
animals and birds, for all his people had been slain or carried off
into slavery. Now he was freer than ever, but freedom had become
suspect to him. He found himself able to converse with the birds,
and learned from them of the ecstasy which comes from fulfilling
the immemorial patterns of destiny. And at last he set forth all
alone, to find what he could of a past to which he might bind
himself.

Faster than the winds I fly
in my shoes of burnished gold,
all in darkness—for I wear
the cloak of darkness fold on fold.

My oaken staff gives me a strength
greater than ten million men;
I can pound your cities flat
and in a day raise them again.

I live alone. I speak to stones,
I sleep with waters, sing with shells;
and I despise you, facile ones
in your accommodating hells.

I stand immortal in the child.
I'm doomed to leave the growing man—
but at his deathbed I return
and let him seize me if he can,

then through last spasms of fear and pain
bear him up, up to life above.
I am the Messenger of God
and unlike God, I need not love.

When the barbarians conquered the ancient Valley of Zair, they slaughtered the peaceful inhabitants and threw their bodies into the huge, deep lake that stretches for many miles to the south. But the waters were medicinal, and the valley people, as they sank slowly from the surface, found themselves healed. They were able to see and breathe, and soon clustered together in little groups at the bottom, calmly discussing what had befallen them. The waters were clear and pleasant, the fish not unfriendly, there were patterns of light and shade, and quiet all about. And so they adapted themselves to their new home, and live there still, leading very long lives, begetting few children, moving slowly, smiling sympathetically to one another—thinking. . . . It is said they will come out of the lake when everyone else in the world is dead.

The two little children who wandered from their home on Christmas Eve, and were lost on the mountain—what became of them? The tiny girl, and her slightly older brother who protected her and held her by the hand? They froze to death. Their little garments of wool were not enough to keep out the bitter cold, and they were lost, lost in the snow, out on the mountainside all night. Their bodies were found the next day. So it was an unhappy ending. Just as all *true* endings are unhappy. Or are they? For, between beginning and ending, who may measure the depths to which we may strike? Depths which may make a mockery of beginning and ending. Who knows what shapes those two saw, as they walked hand in hand through the snow?

THREE

Life is, in itself and for ever, shipwreck.
—*ORTEGA Y GASSET*

I

In Panama, in 1948,
swinging from his jungle reverie
                    onto high-tension wires,
a boa was electrocuted. . . .

Friends, it was the beginning of the end.

I I

Man is the disease of earth,
the tumor that will kill her:
wherever her bright health extends
he and his filth must fill her,

for he has lust insatiable
which he calls sacred need.
Nothing's too ugly or obscene
that satisfies his greed.

His mind, with which he's pleased and proud,
accomplishes this evil
(for it's his body that's from God,
his mind is from the Devil!)—

In sickly haste it vomits out
its deadly novelties,
each one a poisoner of life
fouling its mysteries.

Its final end? The moon, of course,
that sterile desolation—
waterless, plantless, lifeless. Yes,
there is our destination.

III

When the two astronauts, wading heavily through black metallic dust, had at last made the descent between pitted crags and spires to the floor of the hitherto unexplored valley, they were surprised at first to find it the repository for all kinds of lost and dated things from earth. Flags of departed nations (and of present ones), photographs of movie stars from the 20's, prayer-books and books of incantations, tribal fetishes, astrological charts, political manifestoes, scientific predictions and sociological projections. . . . They talked it over a while in their brisk metallic lingo—then fell silent, realizing that here they too had found their resting-place.

IV

Par les champs de lauriers-roses
       dans un temps d'orage
au bruit confus des tambourins
       I set up my menage

in a still grove of beeches where
       winds mask their tragedies
beneath dark glintings of an air
       charged with the time's unease.

It is an age of burning and
       the fume of stricken towns
lends somber fragrance to the frond-
       ed umbra of the boughs

while scatterings of rain descend
       blind with an ashy taste
upon the shadow-riven glades
       and the red leaves' waste.

The fox pursues his ancient ways
       through burdock fields and yarrow
while still at dawn a chant is raised
       by thrush or dusty sparrow

against the earth's long foul decline—
       but what avails the clean
nobility of breathing beasts
       when reason, in serene

splendor of agony and crime
       chars blackly towards death?
The creatures of a murdering time
       draw but despairing breath.

. . . Dear nymph of earth who share my bread
          and deep impassive rest,
the wild bees hum about your head
          and squirrels suck your breasts:

you're made of leaf and rain and soil
          and the strong consciousness
that dwells within the roots of things
          beneath the mind's distress.

Your lips release the time's dull weight
          from my pure-lidded eyes
while the scourged will is rinsed of hate
          between your pliant thighs,

and in our dim gold afternoons
          when by the pool's clear rim
amid the dart of demoiselles
          I breach your sinless womb,

through that strong body clean with lust
          and undimmed violet gaze
I spurn the god whose reeking dust
          begs our immortal praise.

V

Prairies of wildebeest, fat plains of oxen!
Professor Cinq-Mars administers anti-toxin
along the tse-tse belt, down purple savannahs,
to buxom black belles in vegetable bandanas,
thinks, as he inspects the fat ranks of brown titties,
better King Turd than the life of great cities—
late sad stars of the declining west
glowing with *schadenfreude* in their gilded nests.

Meanwhile, half-smiling in languid stealth,
the ghost of Rimbaud rises from the filth
of foul Ethiopia's clotted diseases,
makes for the coast, crosses secret seas
on an unmarked black freighter bound west for New York.
The fate drops anchor. The ghost makes port.
It's springtime. He takes a Saturday walk:
buys a balloon, strolls in Central Park,
admires his reflection in eyes at the zoo,
rubs and enters the bodies on Fifth Avenue;
then goes to his Club, sits at a window alone,
has a drink, and decides which new life he'll put on.

V I

To escape the doom he scraped the sun
taking the trail of the shining one
who left the earth when life was young
a million spawning years ago

and circumventing Betelgeuse
found him a second earth to choose—
all tender greens and fragrant dews—
without a human face to show,

in whose great forests no apes swing
nor monkeys vent their yammerings
nor live such clever, grasping things
as some day into men may grow

but only older, saner stocks:
elephant, tiger, bear and fox
at ease with trees and streams and rocks,
who know but what they need to know.

VII

Invited to dinner by the Prince of the Planet,
we took a small space-ship with a select group.
Paula went topless, in her bright-checked skirt,
I wore a double-breasted, pin-striped suit.

The landscape was rural, much like the Swiss shore
of Lake Geneva, with vineyards above;
the people were strictly stratified by caste
and wore green, red or blue accordingly.

Visitors, we were privileged in that place,
but there was hunger, fighting in the streets.
The Prince, a suave Bolivian type,
had received a love-letter from the Philippines

but when we were asked to translate, we declined
(courteously)—because, as Paula said,
something about it all was not quite right
and there's no end to the favors dreams may seek.

VIII

Tentative
       on the sunny hill
three men of mist
        gaze down the valley.

Blue-robed, they come
        from the blue sky:
their heads contain
        unyielding wisdom.

Comets, planets,
        the vehement stars,
all are controlled by
        knowable powers,

but who shall unfold
        serenities
of white frame house
        tacit in sun—

of man, woman,
        child and brown dog,
and chickens at the back
        of the random garden?

A force is here,
        but a force appeased:
as three heads ponder
        the instant, poised.

I X

A space that stretches back to stars
and tempts your hand with marigolds;
a private space, all elegance
in balancing its own small laws,

where angels sit on river banks
and beasts may come to pay a call
and every night fresh windows open
over prophetic bays of blue:

A demon's rare intelligence
has wrought this strange perfection—see,
within the quiet living space,
his pledge of immortality.

Praise to the spirit who from flux
selects such small things as time gives
and in their cool arrangement tells
our hot world how the mind may live.

(After certain collages by Joseph Cornell)

X

Her arms are muscular, her face is fresh,
she's digging her own grave here in the churchyard.
Sitting on a tombstone at one side,
her silent sister watches with a half-smile.

Sunset. The country air is still:
a blue-gray, quiet evening light.
Two girls—in action, in repose—
shed their inner peace upon this scene.

(After the painting Vale of Rest *by John Everett Millais)*

XI

To the trampling of a thousand horses
September comes
in the stillness of the dead-leaf smoke
of a thousand burnings,
while the swifts dot-and-dash above the barns.

Peace in the fields? Perhaps.
But far from the myth, even,
one thinks of dying and the restless dead
who shift about this world—
and of the older dead not dead at all.

The old woman gathering faggots
in the smoky wood
spoke me the charm one day
at the end of the hedge where the road begins,
one dark day of September:

> *Leaf dies and falls: is burned.*
> *False man, falsely dead,*
> *loses his all-self*
> *in smoke of the underworld.*
> *But true man truly dies*
> *and lives again on the tree.*
> *Child, there is the road.*
> *Find your true destiny.*

XII

A knapsack with some scraps of food was enough to start off with.
Marvels would come just down the road:
an enchanted animal speaking from the forest
or, in the village market square, a wizard in search of a boy.

It was well enough known what qualities were necessary:
endurance, steadfastness, loyalty
and a certain humorous confidence in the nature of things.
Mystery lay beneath the commonplace; but the mystery had a
        pattern

and things always came out right for the one who was true to
        himself.
Great rewards: gold, jewels,
the hand of the princess, a kingdom to rule,
the friendship of animals, long peaceful years of life.

He merited all this by his courage, his cleverness and steadfastness:
and those who failed—who were slain,
or found themselves changed into loathsome serpents
or imprisoned in dark dungeons for centuries—they merited their
        fates,

just because they refused to understand the nature of their world.
Their world—which is our own
when we look deeply through the mirror
and see the dark, undying woods to which our destinies are bound.

XIII

When the old mirror crashed in the ruined castle,
released from long imprisonment in time
a red-haired man stepped forth into the day.

He saw the littered yard, the clumps of weeds,
a road, a house beyond, a child playing,
and vacant fields strewn with forlorn debris

that stretched off in the haze to where the towers
of a huge somber city rose. Time paused—
while the man rubbed his eyes and looked again.

All was quiet, but the child still played.
Far off, a thing flew down the sky, too straight
for any bird. Gone was the castle, gone

the arms and tapestries, and the deep groves
where streams flowed cool and clear through the rich green,
and gone his ancient dreams of good and evil.

... The child ran from him, frightened of his beard.
Lost in the centuries, the man set forth
along the dusty road to find a home.

XIV

I saw a beast's leg in the mirror,
turned—and viewed the empty air.
What was it had been standing there?
I took an hour apart to think.

Projection of my mood, perhaps?
Yet all was still and clear within:
the sudden visitant brought no
strains of emotion from his world.

Was he my foe? With fur so handsome?
Friend? But he showed a shining claw.
The glimmering moment of his time
held neither threat nor consolation.

I said a prayer, and then I knew him,
creature of chance from God's free land,
Angel—bearing no command
but the deep marvel of that instant.

X V

That land is female in its rolling glades,
its acrid thickets and brackish smell of sea.
Entering it by the proper stratagems
one can be rid of the mind's complexity,

shedding that strange external skeleton
which holds the body from its natural bliss:
body sinks naked to the earth, and feels
the earth itself shape it to what it is.

Let body live or die—so it be true,
untyrannized by the mind's anxious laws!
Close to the female, it is close to God:
breasts and womb belong to the First Cause.

A gentle heaven's there for those who'll find it,
demanding, though, the last humility
such that you'll hug the contours of the ground
in desperate gift of your identity.

No separation, no possession, there—
no pride, shame, fearfulness, despair or haste:
but being that in deeper being dwells,
the God within his Consort's arms embraced.

XVI

On the last day,
while the last men were strangling in the slime,
the Centaur, who had kept watch of the years,
looked gravely out once more from Pelion
where a few shrubs still struggled into bloom,
and made the last withdrawal to his cave:
there deep within himself he turned himself
and moved his mind and his twin natures through
a new dimension into the new world,
ready to teach the heroes who might come.

XVII

. . . Caught in the upper reaches of the mantle
and hurtling down a thousand miles per second
burning—then through the canopy of air
more slowly drifting down to a frothing sea. . . .

Plunge. Depths of strange brine. Creatures swallowing
and diving into huger firmaments
below. An enormous gale over that ocean
driving the flotsam in to distant shores.

Touching the rocks and sand: emerging. Scent
of salt and iodine in a clearing mist.
Beneath the sun ten thousand miles of surf
beating on beaches where the forest ends.

FOUR

With these goblet words that come forth day after day, I harmonize all things in the Heavenly Equality, leave them to their endless changes, and so live out my years.

—CHUANG TZU

I

Not by action, bringing about some end,
may we pass from the complexities of self
and touch such true existence as we have,
but, by being ourselves ends here in time—
ends that no doubt must go beyond our thought,
reflecting simply God's still presence here
as myriad waves each mirror the same sun.
The wind's voice whispers to us: "Let it be.
Your destiny is not something to shape
but something to grow into, if you can:
a slow discovery, not to be forced.
And never think you win God's victory
for him: it was won long ago. Refrain;
and find it in yourself by being still."

Dear son, you died three years ago today.
I died too, and have risen from the dead
and take you with me in my blood and bones
through a new life. —Poor boy, what was there left?
Your corpse, part-decomposed when it was found,
sent home for burial; your clothing, books,
letters, snapshots—a suitcaseful shipped home.
Sad remnants, John. But I, your father, knew you
and know you now and through my life shall bear you
in my deep self, remembering your warmth,
your goodness and the radiance of your smile—
yes, bear you in my heart's blood and brain's fiber
until at long last in my turn I'm called
by him who knows us both and knows all men.

III

FOR MARK

Dear brave young man, with courage and with humor
you fought your losing battle to the end.
How did you do it, death being at large
within you, choking off each hope in turn?
Yet deep in pain you ran the bitter course
to its known ending, and maintained your grace.
Some other force was living in your life,
some force that shapes us all, bears us through all—
pain, joy, love, death—and will remember us,
a force that speaks plain words now: "Mark, well done,
well lived."
          Well lived indeed, young man! And I,
who only met you twice, must mourn you still,
untimely snatched from me, my only brother,
for that is what you would have been—and are.

IV

Sometimes at night when I've undressed,
I put my hand against my chest
and feel skin, roughness, hair, the bone beneath,
blood flowing there, heart beating—
and think: I am so precious, I
am the one and only "I";
think too, this will melt away—
if not today, some other day—
what happens then?

Doubtless the small "I" dissolves
into a larger nothing . . .
which may be a larger "I" (no guarantee).
In any case, the evident I
is made of timely things,
knotted and clustered hopes and fears,
which one can start to dissolve immediately
and feel the better for it. Feel free.
To the larger rhythms life moves easily
(and death is part of them), and one forgets the "I"
and grows another being that moves beyond
death and life in natural transition.
"I told myself death is no new, strange thing"
(so said Chuang Tzu)—
indeed it may be an opening,
as Socrates also knew.

V

The wise old man said, "He's a fool
who tries to live his life by rule,
but if you think to get to heaven
by rules, I'll gladly give you seven.

First, *be healthy:* because, you know,
your body's you, it's where you grow
and meet the real world, opening.
Don't treat it like a foreign thing.

Next, *dutiful:* your duty is
to observe the common decencies.
Don't lie, cheat, swindle, injure, kill—
or wish another person ill.
This doesn't mean you have to do
what other people tell you to.

Those two are elementary.
The third may give more difficulty.
It is: *to meditate,* a rule
repulsive to the modern fool,
who doubts his own reality
unless he fidgets endlessly
in mind and body. But, give in!
Sit down, be quiet, look within
and face the nothingness that's there
and learn to make friends with despair.

The fourth rule follows: it's *to pray*—
a little bit, at least, each day—
not to ask favors from some kind
daddy you've pictured in your mind,
nor to propitiate the wrath
of a supernatural psychopath,

but to maintain your own true being
by sinking to the deepest seeing
and touching once again the great
Source from which beings emanate:
for meditation takes you where
the only step beyond is prayer.

Returning then to life and choice,
follow the fifth rule, *to rejoice*—
not just in pleasant, happy things
but in whatever fortune brings.
Seize life, enjoy it: days and nights,
all pleasures, friendships and delights;
but even when it's time to part,
let there be springtime in your heart.

Sixth rule: *to serve*—to serve all others
as your true-born sisters and brothers,
sprung from one Source, to It returning.
Please, without fuss. Don't think you're earning
merit, distinction or acclaim.
Don't even think of your own name,
but let all happen naturally
as rivers flowing to the sea.

The seventh, last and greatest: *Love!*
which means all this I've spoken of
and more besides, which can't be told.
You'll find it, maybe, if you hold
to the first six most faithfully;
then all unravels, clear and free,
into one calm simplicity."

Those were the words of that old man,
let him make sense of them who can.
There's no fool like a wise old man.

V I

PAIN POEMS

1

At first it seems impossible, unreal—
not to be admitted or recognized—
as though only by some insane mistake
this thing had been allowed within the gates.
That's when it's hardest, that's when not to panic
but look within and center yourself within,
immerse yourself in it and ride the waves
borne up by your own strength, which now you will
learn intimately along with the pain.
Strange, is it not, that it should be through pain
that men and women come to know themselves
deeply—I'll not say most deeply of all—
but very deeply? It's a challenge to us.
And this is where the Cross has relevance.

2

In last extremities of pain and fear
when you are all alone with nothingness
and clench your teeth on it and taste despair,
if you remember this is each man's fate
and God's fate, too, as far as we are he,
and let your inner substance rest on it
and merge with it, as with a summer sea—
then comes the Change. You have become the pain
and all at once attained the further shore.
This is the meaning of the Crucified:

not to adore your pain but feel through it
until you reach the country that's beyond,
where you may touch the liberated One
eternally rejoicing to be found.

3

The carcass of a man impaled by spikes
upon a wooden frame, all soaked in blood,
smelling of blood and pain in the noonday sun—
an ugly thing to worship, you will say.
Ugly indeed, if it's the blood and pain
we yearn for in a sick desire of soul,
loathing our bodies, fearing our full selves—
and this has been, for most, the Christian way.
But there's another way to look at it:
this poor thing that has suffered and has died
need not be ugly if it's simply seen
as bodying an aspect of our being
that's inescapable and binds us all.
We're vulnerable; we're mortal; we must love.

4

Pain is to be avoided nowadays
if one possibly can. That's natural.
What isn't natural is to deny it
when it's right there inside, or to pretend
that somehow it's a thing to be ashamed of.

For pain itself is natural in its time
as much as pleasure is: if you feel one,
the ground's prepared to feel the other, too.
True pain, true pleasure have a valid life
that gives the inner being discipline,
but those who fear to feel with their full selves
pursue unreal pleasures and are pursued
by fears of unreal pain: an equal torment.
True pain would save them if they'd let it in.

5

If you must have an image for your worship,
better a naked woman than this victim,
for see her as you wish—chaste and serene,
lascivious, enticing or obscene—
she still is gift of life, pledge of fruition;
this punctured man seems nothing but defeat.
There is a rhythm though in the way of things
that balances fulfillment with despair,
helps us to see that neither one is final
and points to a freedom that's beyond them both,
fulfillment past fulfillment and despair.
We'd take the woman then if we had to choose,
but the great dance encompasses the two.
Truth is, we had better keep them both in mind.

VII

Good days, bad days alternate;
tragedies and joys.
Take them not too seriously
nor let them break your poise.
What *you* are dies, dies each day,
drawn back into the stream;
what you *are* survives, deep under day,
flowing with the stream.
Angry, fearful, pained—pull back
your senses from their riot,
close ears and eyes, correct yourself
in darkness and in quiet.

VIII

Time was, seeing that blonde pass by
I'd put myself between her thighs
thinking, overanxiously,
each girl a willing lap for me.

It's different now. Those other charms
draw me more surely to your arms—
and random lusts that once I knew
all merge in my deep thirst for you.

I X

If it rains,
   it's all right!
If I die today,
   all right—
Things go on,
   sun and rain,
etcetera.
   I'm a part of them.

X

Walking the edge of the precipice
each day, facing the last abyss?

Yes.

How fearful. It's the end of hope,
of happiness—the end of life.

No.

How do you bear the terror?

As joy—
for freedom turns all into joy
as we merge with our destinies.
Then it's blessing unspeakable
to know the world wherein we dwell,
see with final clarity
death and life as unity,
and—ready to give our selves away—
strong and simple greet each day.

X I

Let no woman disdain
        nor man hinder me,
a knower of magic
        and dweller by the shore of the sea.

XII

Swift horse of the moon,
watch over this house,
this house on the water,
this home under stars.

Proud prow of night,
look up at the stars!
There you course
when the moon is bright,

dark wind in your mane,
space a-hum in your ears—
you draw the goddess
through oncoming years

yourself elemental
wind-animal-god,
dweller at the crossing
of the mind's three roads—

watch over this house,
let no evil approach,
and only such pain
as the moon bears away.

XIII

SONG

Clear-shining moon,
you make radiant the night.

Yes, moon, clear-shining
silvery-white,
night-long shed your light
where my dear one lies sleeping—
where naked she shines
and makes radiant the night.

(From the Spanish, XVth century, anonymous)

XIV

Sir Hummingbird dips his long spear
into the golden honeycups
and out again, then whirs away
across the garden at mid-day.
Soon he returns; and darts and stops,
tasting his favorites once more.

The while our honeysuckle vine
remains in bloom, he'll keep this up.
He starts at dawn. We lie adrowse
in our big bed and hear him come,
blending his low and vibrant hum
with the soft droning of the bees.

Until, one day, he'll disappear
and stay away until next year.
I have no notion where he goes.
And some day, too, he'll die, and drop
small and stiff to the earth, and rot.
Meanwhile, what beauty is like his?

X V

The wild ones kept their code of kill and eat.
They did not need to feel themselves, or grow;
and held their honor till they died. But we,
race of sad apes grown sensitive and smart,
think that by thinking we shall know the world.
Sad error, since the world as object known
ever recedes beyond our nervous grasp:
the very thinking pushes it away.
Whereas, if we were part of it, we'd know it—
as the wild ones did and do, who are dying now.

XVI

A thousand things, a thousand beings, live inside me.
I shall not subdue them, like "unruly horses"
(that was the old way), nor—in the newer fashion—
surrender my sense of a distinct responsibility:

not to be ruler, that is, but as a mediator
somehow to gain the trust of these strong, stubborn creatures,
who have such tendencies to pride and childish demanding
that sometimes, for all our thought, there are painful collisions.

Yet mostly, we seek harmony, with a friendly give-and-take
and as much understanding as all of us can muster.
It helps to know that in the end we are all expressions of God:
ripples and cross-ripples on the one mighty ocean.

XVII

Shedding the False one—what a chore!
He may crawl back in any shape.
But you will know him from the furtive
clinging stink of nervous ape.

XVIII

One could be happy, if one had the courage
just to say no to all except one's self;
provided this were the true secret self
and not a costume such as most selves are.
In saying yes to *this,* one reaffirms
a love for all the multitudes of being
and solidarity with things and lives
and the dark sacred soil that lies beneath.
Hard, though, to find this self: one knocks about,
muddling one's life with various encounters,
burdens, responsibilities and joys,
until it seems all strength of sight has gone.
But it's still there—like a lost inner eye
that opens when the outer eyes have closed.

XIX

He thought he'd made his bet and lost.
He died, was buried; after a while
found he was but a feeble ghost
unable to feel things that were real.

He moved about unhappily
trying to touch the ones he'd lost—
without success. He had no touch,
no way of reaching to the past,

only could see, as through a fog,
dear faces fading in the dark.
Then he stood still, and looked inside,
and saw, where his heart beat, a spark

that rose in silence to the east
and brightened hugely on the air;
then, quietly, he was released
into sheer presence everywhere.

He was himself, he was all else,
he was more still, not to be told . . .
The mists were rising all about.
The sun came up on a new world.

XX

I have become a child again—
thank the dear Lord, thank the dear Lord—
I have become a child again,
thank the dear Lord who made me.

Those words were in my heart today
when I awoke. Why should this be?
Because I sensed within myself
a new and strange transparency,

an instinct that, were I to feel
pain, anger, joy, fear or desire,
I'd know at once the source of it,
as, from its heat, a child knows fire.

No more the sick unease that comes
when passion fears, and seeks disguise
(the child's reward who's taught to live
appeasing other people's lies),

but each emotion flowing pure,
undeviant, from its pure source,
as a clear stream, unhindered, flows
now wild, now gentle, on its course.

It's God who brought the change about.
He took from me my own dear son—
a young and ardent life it was—
but then he gave me back my own

and gave me, too, another life,
a woman's life fast-joined to mine
as lover, comrade, friend and wife—
there never was a gift so fine—

and in our larger life I have
my deep and hidden self regained.
So, all this change, and pain, and love
have freed me from my ancient chains

and here, now, in my fiftieth year,
when many lives I know have ceased,
I have become a child again—
a child of many memories.

Even my body's new and strange!
Who can foresee the ways of God?
I've further still to go, I think,
but now, at least, I'm on the road.

I have become a child again—
thank the dear Lord, thank the dear Lord—
I have become a child again,
thank the dear Lord who made me.

XXI

Plato? He may be wrong or right,
but there *is* an ideal Paula
for ever beautiful and good:
the same Paula who's here each day.

XXII

The other morning I awoke from a dream with the sound in my ears of tires coming to rest in soft gravel. I had been carried gently forward, in a slumber; I sensed sunlight and warmth just outside; as the motion stopped a voice spoke to me: "Here we are, Mr. Frederick."

I awoke, at peace, in the present. But the images were from forty years ago, from a Connecticut summer of my boyhood. We had been out for a ride, or were returning from the beach; I had fallen asleep in the back seat; and now the car had pulled up before our front door, and all was quiet in the late afternoon sunlight as the chauffeur—or perhaps it was my governess—announced our return. I would step from the car and see the wide green lawn (on which the sprinkler would be revolving), the flower-beds, and tall and handsome trees. I would pause a moment, to see where the sun hung low over distant woods, and then pass through the familiar doorway into the white, dimly lit house, where downstairs my grandmother would be taking her tea, and upstairs my much-loved room awaited me.

The voice in the dream may have been a servant's, but it was in no way humble. Rather, it was the voice of one who knew me well, who had been with us a long time. Friendly, independent, from a world of its own; but acknowledging me, the child, as heir of mine.

Strange, the solidity and rightness of this dream. As though in all travels, through many lives and many selves, one is never very far from the destination—which, indeed, one may come to, even after the greatest apparent dislocations, quietly as at the end of a summer day. The child within is never far away. And within the child's self is another, more profound, more immediate life.

Let me live to be a hundred—the end will not be very different. The strange, enduring, friendly, impersonal voice. "Here we are, Mr. Frederick." Where? At the house we have always known, where the First Persons dwell.

XXIII

As, in the gardens of the dead,
the amaranth blooms on unfading,
so, John, within my mind's deep realms
you live, and live, and live, for ever.

XXIV

The freight trains
       in the days of my youth
were Satan's bones
shaking in ecstasy—

as the child loves
       what is forbidden
and fears it, too:
that joy of other lives.

Nights of July,
       Connecticut nights,
the summertime earth
sweet in my nostrils,

I thought of girls
       with strange yellow hair,
of dark towns under
the dark night sky

where men watched alone
       in diners, in bars,
under bare lights
in the smell of stations

while trains rumbled out,
       slumbrously tugging,
into deep night . . .
I thought of them waiting—

I, in my bed
       alone, all alone,
not knowing the world
nor where was my home.

XXV

Skipping stones down on my shore
I thought of you, good cousin;
sometimes I get just one big leap,
sometimes a skimming dozen.

We played this game when we were boys.
Now we are somewhat older,
but one thing can't be said of us:
that our hearts grew colder.

XXVI

AUGUST

1

On an August evening
        through dusk of shrubs and trees
the girl and I walked outside hand in hand,

and lay in the long grass
        of a soft, fresh-mown field
while the night insects uttered their low spells.

She leaned long above me;
        I felt her breasts' fullness
and the slow sweat that started from her flanks . . .

My sex in her soft center,
        beyond her hair—the stars!
. . . Eternal moment lost, still to be found.

2

Cicada, harvest-fly, you come
        out in the days of the dog—
your males emit the vibrant hum
of timelessness in August fields
now as in my boyhood days
when I thought time had no end . . . .

Imagos imbibe sap of trees.
Nymphs live in soil, suck sap from roots,
after seventeen secret years
assume their brief maturity.

3

Ninety degrees of August heat!
Naked we run along the shore
crowning ourselves with sea-weed wreaths
and splash, laugh, touch—adore.

4

Via lactea, luminous belt of light
        "composed of countless worlds,"
in your slow turn you bless this night—
yes, in that silent turning of a quarter billion years,
        one round of the celestial sphere,
you bless, and bless again, the August night.

XXVII

Great hooks baited with living flesh
at times draw up Leviathan,
Jehovah's scaled and scowling pet,
or the Snake Thor went fishing for.

Better not reach or try to grasp
but let the biters swim to you.
Be sure, once the life's line is cast,
soon or late the huge pull will come.

Best of all, to wander free,
detached from God, without a goal,
and find among archaic rocks
his word tossed up upon the shore.

XXVIII

Frail bark! launched on these mountain waves:
late or soon, it will founder.
Love it, but place no trust in it.
Trust only the waves that will drown you.

XXIX

Into the night,
        Dolores,
you take your flight,
insect of death. . . .

Horror of the
        grave abates
in the dawn's red
stain fresh-blooming.

How shall the ghost
        return, then,
but to the great
earth-spirit's side?

Metal, stone, weeds—
        the rich spawn
phosphorescent
under the waves

lead the freed mind
        beyond sense
of pain recur-
rent unto death.

XXX

Death, from where we stand, is nonexistence;
but from another standpoint *here* is unreal,
the wrong side of the tapestry—where work is done
that only shows its form on the other side.

Dreams give a sense of this. There is a meaning
that holds us while we're there as part of itself,
but which we lose on the way back. We wake,
feeling deprived of a larger understanding.

Imagine yourself in a huge dark mansion
at night: you're not quite lost, not quite at home,
and free, or so it seems, to move about.
Rooms, halls and stairways, all are still and dark

and yet you know that in that very house
a party is planned and guests are gathering—
talking, laughing, filling the bright-lit rooms—
but you can't find them. —That's the situation.

XXXI

Although he deals hard blows and gives great boons,
God does not wish to punish or reward
as though he sat with answers in his hand
waiting to mark us either sheep or goat.
It's not so simple. Somehow he's mixed up
in all this with us; cares, participates,
while holding all the while his ancient realm
that goes beyond our knowledge now. This, though,
we may share with him, if we let ourselves,
as he shares our flesh when we deeply know.
Yes—what befalls us here is part of him,
and what we make of it is part as well,
and through this painful sharing, which is love,
he works within us to establish meaning.

XXXII

"Vanishing backward
      from your own skull
see it go,
      that I you thought was 'I.' "

*

Stands of caribou
      in Alaska:
brown eyes look upward
      at the dawn of death—

all are contained in
      the "I" of Alaska,
the "I" of caribou,
      the "I" of death.

*

What god lives in the breaking wave?
What is the "moment" of a mind?
Where is a birth from? And why?
You see, do you not, the hinge?

*

Before her hidden cave
      that overlooks blue waters
the Vola remembers
      days that will come

for gods slay each other
            but mind foresees
eternal rebirth
            of what "now" is.

*

"Are you withdrawn now
            back into my Presence?
Has it gone,
            that 'I' you thought was I?"

XXXIII

Letting go into God is almost physical;
is physical, really, if you put your mind to it,
like letting your body slide into a quarry pool
deep in the woods. It's summertime—hot sun, green trees—
but the water is dark and chill, and there is no one watching.
You slip from the edge—a shock of cold—and then you're free!
Indeed, if you died that instant, free for ever
because you've given your self.
                              That's what each living moment
is, in a life, if you come down to it.
But we forget, because we're caught up in the network
of hopes, desires, fears—and because we try
to live in an illusion of permanence.
God tells us to be mindful of the physical:
the self is cunning, and will play its pleasant games
as long as we allow. But the heart stops at last.
The truth is in the shock and the surrender.

XXXIV

The devastation
    of being
    brings being
    more newly—

the harp
    of creation
    may reverberate
    more truly

when the great
    final wind
    blows strong
    through its branches

and the soul
    pale and brave
    to its first home
    advances.

XXXV

Shakespeare said it: The readiness is all.
When the fruit is ripe, it's ready to fall.
Fear, bitter fear, that you die unready—
So let the life come, hold yourself steady,
save the inner dark for the destined germ,
let the inner meaning reach its full term
of natural growth, whatever the cost;
do not hasten it, or all may be lost.
Hold fast to this, and there is no more fear,
whatever of pain there may be to bear.
Do what you must; then, ready to depart,
with a whole life's fullness brimming in your heart,
die. And be born? That's as it may befall.
Now is this word: that the ripeness is all.

XXXVI

I had no time, for twenty-five years,
to pause and take stock of my growth,
to learn of my own hidden ways,
the give-and-take of powers within.

Always an outer need compelled me—
or so I thought, or so I made it—
to fix on parent, wife or child
the energies that were all mine.

Many demands, of course, were just.
Loving dependence has its rights.
Still, if a man would be himself,
he must not let it all be claimed.

I almost did, and almost lost.
Thank God, who saved me ruthlessly,
gave me another chance to find
what I am, what I may be—

gave me Paula, who long ago
knew the truth that I've just learned:
it's only when you have yourself
that you can share yourself in love.

XXXVII

If I die, I die with you,
        trees and growing things,
perhaps to grow again with flowers
        or seeds or wings,
perhaps to be consumed within
        more savage life
or joined for good with that which lives
        beyond all life;
no matter: to have lived a length
        of the great being,
to have half-seen, once or twice,
        what passes seeing,
to feel, within, the carnivore's
        strong, acrid stain
fade as autumn colors fade
        in the wintry rain—
this is the deep ardor which
        I daily taste,
slowly growing, slowly purging
        fear and hate and haste.

XXXVIII

A prayer a day
      a poem a day
when my goblet brims
      I tilt it gently
pour my libation to the ground
the sacred web from which we grow

When it's empty
      empty and dry
I shut my eyes
      quiet my thoughts
and let it fill invisibly
from secret sources self-sustained

Giving, taking
      dying, living
that's the rhythm
      the way things go
the single life in balance moving
through the ten thousand shapes of time

XXXIX

After twenty-five years
        to be in touch with myself
to bring it all together and, what's more, to love—

this is ripeness, the golden fruit
of the great world-tree that dies, and lives.